Life Skills Series

Bull   flict

Blackburn
College

Library
01254 292120

Please return this book on or before the last date below

25/09/18

g at school
esolution
solving

By Jane Bourke

D1477597

KS2/3

Life Skills Series
Bullying and Conflict
(BLM)

© 2010 Aber Education by agreement with Ready-Ed Publications
Printed in Europe

ISBN: 978-1-84285-179-1

Author: Jane Bourke
additional material Dr Graham Lawler
Typesetting & Design: Shay Howard and Aber Publishing
Artwork: Terry Allen

The advice mentioned in this book is given in good faith. The author and the publishers and their agents cannot be held acountable for outcomes related to activities mentioned herein

Published by:
Aber Education
P.O. Box 225
Abergele
Conwy County LL18 9AY

Aber Education

•Contents•

•About the Life Skills Series•

This series aims to provide the busy classroom teacher with practical ideas and strategies for developing and enhancing a set of valuable life skills in individual students.

There are numerous resources and articles about teaching values, dealing with grief, addressing bullying and the like, however, most of these articles and programs outline strategies for dealing with the problem at the whole-school level. While this is indeed a very appropriate way to deal with such matters, it has become obvious that there is a lack of ready-to-use materials for the actual classroom teacher. The Life Skills Series aims to fill the gap between the frameworks set out by national bodies and the delivery of practical and meaningful lessons in the classroom.

The Life Skills Series comprises four books:

Self Esteem and Values

- Enhancing self esteem of individuals
- Developing an awareness of feelings
- Promoting realistic goal-setting
- Enriching values in the classroom and community

Bullying and Conflict

- Coping with bullying at school
- Exploring conflict resolution through a problem solving approach

Grief, Illness and Other Issues

- Coping with grief and loss
- Dealing with a disability or serious illness

Family Relationships

- Discussing family roles
- Dealing with anger and other emotions
- Coping with separation, divorce and conflict

Each of the books in this series should be used as required. The series is not structured to be a complete program of work. Instead, it is designed as a valuable and practical resource for teachers that find themselves with students who are going through difficult life events.

Most of the activities are stand-alone – it is up to the teacher to decide what sheets will be relevant to the class. Some sheets will only be relevant to a select number of students, e.g. a bereaved student or a student who belongs to a blended family.

The themes in these four books overlap and so, when dealing with a particular issue, e.g. conflict resolution, activities from other books in this series might also be relevant to the situation that may exist in your classroom.

As well as student worksheets, all books contain extensive background notes for teachers, parents and students. Several sections contain annotated guides to relevant websites and literature resources available both online and in hard copy. Also included are extension ideas and teaching ideas for the classroom. The activities are linked to relevant student outcomes (see Pages 5-9) for all areas of the UK

Internet References

Websites that are included in these four books can be accessed easily by visiting:

www.aber-publishing.co.uk

Bookmark this page for ease of use. To notify of any broken links e-mail info@aber-publishing. co.uk

•Curriculum Links•

National Curriculum England

The importance of personal, social and health education and citizenship

Personal, social and health education (PSHE) and citizenship help to give pupils the knowledge, skills and understanding they need to lead confident, healthy, independent lives and to become informed, active, responsible citizens. Pupils are encouraged to take part in a wide range of activities and experiences across and beyond the curriculum, contributing fully to the life of their school and communities. In doing so they learn to recognise their own worth, work well with others and become increasingly responsible for their own learning. They reflect on their experiences and understand how they are developing personally and socially, tackling many of the spiritual, moral, social and cultural issues that are part of growing up. They also find out about the main political and social institutions that affect their lives and about their responsibilities, rights and duties as individuals and members of communities. They learn to understand and respect our common humanity, diversity and differences so that they can go on to form the effective, fulfilling relationships that are an essential part of life and learning.

Key stage 3

During key stage 3 pupils learn about themselves as growing and changing individuals and as members of their communities with more maturity, independence and power. They become more self-aware, and are capable of more sophisticated moral reasoning. They take more responsibility for themselves and become more aware of the views, needs and rights of people of all ages. They build on the experience, confidence and competence they developed in key stage 2, learning new skills to help them make decisions and play an active part in their personal and social life. They learn how to plan and manage choices for their courses and career. They continue to develop and maintain a healthy lifestyle, coping well with their changing bodies and feelings. They also learn to cope with changing relationships and understand how these can affect their health and well-being. They make the most of new opportunities to take part in the life of the school and its communities.

Knowledge, skills and understanding

Developing confidence and responsibility and making the most of their abilities

1. Pupils should be taught:
   a) to reflect on and assess their strengths in relation to personality, work and leisure
   b) to respect the differences between people as they develop their own sense of identity
   c) to recognise how others see them, and be able to give and receive constructive feedback and praise
   d) to recognise the stages of emotions associated with loss and change caused by death, divorce, separation and new family members, and how to deal positively with the strength of their feelings in different situations
   e) to relate job opportunities to their personal qualifications and skills, and understand how the choices they will make at key stage 4 should be based not only on knowledge of their personal strengths and aptitudes, but also on the changing world of work
   f) to plan realistic targets for key stage 4, seeking out information and asking for help with career plans
   g) what influences how we spend or save money and how to become competent at managing personal money.

Developing a healthy, safer lifestyle

2. Pupils should be taught:
   a) to recognise the physical and emotional changes that take place at puberty and how to manage these changes in a positive way
   b) how to keep healthy and what influences health, including the media
   c) that good relationships and an appropriate balance between work, leisure and exercise can promote physical and mental health
   d) basic facts and laws, including school rules, about alcohol and tobacco, illegal substances and the risks of misusing prescribed drugs
   e) in a context of the importance of relationships, about human reproduction, contraception, sexually transmitted infections, HIV and high-risk behaviours including early sexual activity
   f) to recognise and manage risk and make safer choices about healthy lifestyles, different environments and travel
   g) to recognise when pressure from others threatens their personal safety and well-being, and to develop effective ways of resisting pressures, including knowing when and where to get help
   h) basic emergency aid procedures and where to get help and support.

Developing good relationships and respecting the differences between people

3. Pupils should be taught:
   a) about the effects of all types of stereotyping, prejudice, bullying, racism and discrimination and how to challenge them assertively
   b) how to empathise with people different from themselves
   c) about the nature of friendship and how to make and keep friends
   d) to recognise some of the cultural norms in society, including the range of lifestyles and relationships
   e) the changing nature of, and pressure on, relationships with friends and family, and when and how to seek help
   f) about the role and importance of marriage in family relationships
   g) about the role and feelings of parents and carers and the value of family life
   h) to recognise that goodwill is essential to positive and constructive relationships
   i) to negotiate within relationships, recognising that actions have consequences, and when and how to make compromises

j) to resist pressure to do wrong, to recognise when others need help and how to support them

k) to communicate confidently with their peers and adults.

Breadth of opportunities

4. During the key stage, pupils should be taught the Knowledge, skills and understanding through opportunities to:
   a) take responsibility [for example, for carrying out tasks and meeting deadlines such as taking assembly, running the school newspaper]
   b) feel positive about themselves [for example, by taking part in a public performance]
   c) participate [for example, in developing and putting into practice school policies about anti-bullying; in an action research project designed to reduce crime and improve personal safety in their neighbourhood]
   d) make real choices and decisions [for example, about options for their future, based on their own research and career portfolios]
   e) meet and work with people [for example, people who can give them reliable information about health and safety issues, such as school nurses, community drug awareness workers]
   f) develop relationships [for example, by working together in a range of groups and social settings with their peers and others; by being responsible for a mini-enterprise scheme as part of a small group]
   g) consider social and moral dilemmas [for example, how the choices they make as consumers affect other people's economies and environments]
   h) find information and advice [for example, about the risks of early sexual activity, drug misuse, self-defence for keeping safe]
   i) prepare for change [for example, by anticipating problems caused by changing family relationships and friendships, and by preparing for new styles of learning at key stage 4].

Key stage 4

During key stage 4 pupils use the knowledge, skills and understanding that they have gained in earlier key stages and their own experience to take new and more adult roles in school and the wider community. They develop the self-awareness and confidence needed for adult life, further learning and work. They have opportunities to show that they can take responsibility for their own learning and career choices by setting personal targets and planning to meet them. They develop their ability to weigh up alternative courses of action for health and well-being. They gain greater knowledge and understanding of spiritual, moral, social and cultural issues through increased moral reasoning, clarifying their opinions and attitudes in discussions with their peers and informed adults and considering the consequences of their decisions. They learn to understand and value relationships with a wide range of people and gain the knowledge and skills to seek advice about these and other personal issues. They learn to respect the views, needs and rights of people of all ages.

Knowledge, skills and understanding

Developing confidence and responsibility and making the most of their abilities

1. Pupils should be taught:
   a) to be aware of and assess their personal qualities, skills, achievements and potential, so that they can set personal goals
   b) to have a sense of their own identity and present themselves confidently in a range of situations
   c) to be aware of how others see them, manage praise and criticism, and success and failure in a positive way and learn from the experience
   d) to recognise influences, pressures and sources of help and respond to them appropriately
   e) to use a range of financial tools and services, including budgeting and saving, in managing personal money
   f) about the options open to them post-16, including employment and continuing education and training, and about their financial implications
   g) to use the careers service to help them choose their next steps, negotiate and plan their post-16 choices with parents and others, develop career management skills, and prepare and put into practice personal action plans.

Developing a healthy, safer lifestyle

2. Pupils should be taught:
   a) to think about the alternatives and long- and short-term consequences when making decisions about personal health
   b) to use assertiveness skills to resist unhelpful pressure
   c) the causes, symptoms and treatments for stress and depression, and to identify strategies for prevention and management
   d) about the link between eating patterns and self-image, including eating disorders
   e) about the health risks of alcohol, tobacco and other drug use, early sexual activity and pregnancy, different food choices and sunbathing, and about safer choices they can make
   f) in the context of the importance of relationships, how different forms of contraception work, and where to get advice, in order to inform future choices
   g) to seek professional advice confidently and find information about health
   h) to recognise and follow health and safety requirements and develop the skills to cope with emergency situations that require basic aid procedures, including resuscitation techniques.

Developing good relationships and respecting the differences between people

3. Pupils should be taught:
   a) about the diversity of different ethnic groups and the power of prejudice
   b) to be aware of exploitation in relationships
   c) to challenge offending behaviour, prejudice, bullying, racism and discrimination assertively and take the initiative in giving and receiving support
   d) to work cooperatively with a range of people who are different from themselves
   e) to be able to talk about relationships and feelings
   f) to deal with changing relationships in a positive way, showing goodwill to others and using strategies to resolve disagreements peacefully

g) about the nature and importance of marriage for family life and bringing up children

h) about the role and responsibilities of a parent, and the qualities of good parenting and its value to family life

i) about the impact of separation, divorce and bereavement on families and how to adapt to changing circumstances

j) to know about the statutory and voluntary organisations that support relationships in crisis

k) to develop working relationships with a range of adults, including people they meet during work experience, personal guidance and community activities.

Breadth of opportunities

4. During the key stage, pupils should be taught the Knowledge, skills and understanding through opportunities to:

a) take responsibility [for example, by representing the school to visitors and at outside events]

b) feel positive about themselves [for example, by gaining recognition for the role they play in school life, such as organising activities for younger pupils or working in a resource centre]

c) participate [for example, in an initiative to improve their local community; in challenging activities involving physical performance, public performance or organised events outside the school]

d) make real choices and decisions [for example, about their priorities, plans and use of time; about their choices post-16, with regular review and support]

e) meet and workwith people [for example, through activities such as work experience and industry days; through having an employer as a mentor]

f) develop relationships [for example, by discussing relationships in single and mixed sex groups]

g) consider social and moral dilemmas [for example, young parenthood, genetic engineering, attitudes to the law]

h) find information and provide advice [for example, by providing peer support services to other pupils]

i) prepare for change [for example, in relation to progression to further education and training].

Scotland

As a result of their learning experiences, young people should become progressively more able to demonstrate understanding of:

- contemporary local and global issues, paying regard to available evidence,and to a range of ideas and interpretations of their significance
- the rights and responsibilities underpinning democratic and other societies
- opportunities for individuals and voluntary groups to bring about social and environmental change, and the values on which such endeavours are based
- people's material and spiritual needs and wants and the implications of these for issues such as environmental sustainability and social justice
- the working of the economy, including mechanisms for the creation and uses of wealth
- the causes of conflict and possible approaches to resolving it, recognising that controversy is normal in society and sometimes has beneficial effects
- the barriers to full opportunity to exercise citizenship arising from socioeconomic circumstances, prejudice and discrimination
- decision making processes in society and the roles of the media and marketing in these processes
- global interdependence, and the effects of globalisation on human societies.

Education for citizenship involves developing a range of generic skills, including 'core skills' that are widely recognised as also being essential for personally rewarding living and for productive employment.2 'Competence' is used here to denote a cluster of generic skills that need to be developed along with various personal qualities such as self-esteem, confidence, initiative, determination and emotional maturity in order to be responsible and effective participants in a community. Being skilled and competent as a citizen means feeling empowered, knowing and valuing one's potential for positive action and being generally prepared to take a constructive and proactive approach to issues and problems. Whilst the skills described here may be acquired across a wide range of curricular areas, it is necessary that some explicit links are made with the nature and purpose of education for citizenship.

As a result of their learning experiences, young people should become progressively more able to:

- work independently and in collaboration with others to complete tasks requiring individual or group effort as appropriate
- locate, handle, use and communicate information and ideas, using ICT as appropriate
- question and respond constructively to the ideas and actions of others in debate and/or in writing
- contribute to discussions and debate in ways that are assertive and, at the same time, attentive to and respectful of others' contributions
- make informed decisions in relation to political, community and environmental issues
- persevere, where appropriate, in the face of setbacks and practical difficulties
- negotiate, compromise, or assist others to understand and respect difference, when conflict occurs, recognising the difference between consensus and compliance.

Values and dispositions

A key part of education for citizenship is developing the ability to recognise and respond thoughtfully to values and value judgements that are part and parcel of political, economic, social and cultural life. At the same time, early education centres and schools can help to foster in young people a number of personal qualities and dispositions rooted in values of respect and care for self, for others and for the environment. They can also promote a sense of social responsibility. Being fair-minded in making decisions and being inclined to exercise responsibility are essential qualities of a responsible citizen.

As a result of their learning experiences, young people should become progressively more disposed to:
- develop informed and reasoned opinions about political, economic, social and environmental issues
- express, explain and critically evaluate views that are not their own
- demonstrate a sense of responsibility for the welfare of their communities
- understand and value cultural and community diversity and be respectful of other people
- understand how ethics and values influence people's decisions and actions
- understand and value social justice, recognising that what counts as social justice is itself contentious
- confront views and actions that are harmful to the wellbeing of individuals and communities.

Creativity and enterprise

Being an effective citizen means being able to demonstrate the capacity for thinking and acting creatively in political, economic, social and cultural life. Creative and enterprising citizenship involves making thoughtful and imaginative decisions and being enterprising in one's approach to participation in society. Examples of learning outcomes related to creativity and enterprise for citizenship

As a result of their learning experiences, young people should become progressively more able to:
- identify and frame their own questions and problems and suggest possible solutions
- respond in imaginative ways to social, moral and political dilemmas and challenges
- apply knowledge and skills gained in one context to another in order to take advantage of an opportunity, solve a problem or resolve an issue
- imagine alternatives to current ways of doing things
- manage change, dealing with risk and uncertainty in an enterprising manner
- explore and reach an understanding of their own creative abilities and how to make best use of these.

Wales

PERSONAL & SOCIAL EDUCATION
Outcomes in the Key Concepts
Schools in Wales are now required to provide Personal and Social Education for all registered pupils of compulsory school age. Schools should base their provision on the PSE Framework published by ACCAC in 2000. PSE is a common requirement running through all the national curriculum subjects. Pupils can work towards the learning outcomes below, in relation to Education for Global Citizenship, not just in timetabled 'PSE lessons' but in all subjects – as indicated elsewhere in this Curriculum Map. Pupils acquire knowledge, skills and values relevant to numerous Key Concepts such as Interdependence, Sustainable change, Quality of Life, Diversity, Needs and Rights and Uncertainty and Precaution.

Knowledge: understanding of the universality of human rights and needs

Values: recognise that they have an active role to play in their communities and the wider world

Skills: be aware of their own and other people's views, needs and rights and develop their ability to empathise with others experiences and feelings
Using the subject content
In PSE pupils develop:

Attitudes & Values
Pupils should value cultural diversity and respect other people, e.g. pupils might prepare project: 'the World tomorrow' – a written form, digital message, story telling etc. What can I do today to change/influence tomorrow?
They might focus on human/cultural change, environment and/or personal aspects

Skills
Pupils should be able to express their own views and listen to others' viewpoints e.g. how other cultures pay respect to others, who speaks first when and why? How different rules/customs influence the communication?
They will need to resolve conflict and negotiate agreement, taking into consideration different views and opinions.

Knowledge & Understanding
Pupils should be aware of other cultures, contemporary issues and environment e.g. Pupils might collect information, messages from media and look for stereotypes and prejudice. Why do these e exist? How can we challenge them?

Learning Outcomes from the ACCAC Framework that are particularly relevant to Education for Global Citizenship are set out below:
Key Stage 3/4 **Attitudes and values:**
- Show care and consideration for others and their property and be sensitive towards their feelings.
- Have respect for themselves and others.
- Value cultural diversity and equal opportunity and respect the dignity of all.
- Be disciplined and take responsibility for actions and decisions.
- Be moved by injustice, exploitation and denial of human rights.
- Develop a sense of personal responsibility towards the environment and a concern for the quality of life both in the present and the future.
- Have a sense of personal responsibility towards the environment and be committed to live and act sustainable (KS4)

Skills:
- Communicate confidently one's feelings and views and maintain with conviction a personal standpoint.
- Critically evaluate others' viewpoints and messages from the media.
- Appreciate, reflect on and critically evaluate another person's point of view. (KS4)

- Empathise with others' experiences and feelings.
- Use a range of strategies to resolve conflict.
- Make moral judgements and resolve moral issues and dilemmas.
- Make reasoned judgements.
- Take part in debates and vote on issues.

Knowledge and understanding:Social Aspect
- Understand cultural differences and recognise expressions of prejudice and stereotyping.
- Recognise and know how to challenge expressions of prejudice and stereotyping. (KS4)

Community Aspect
- Understand the nature of local, national and international communities with reference to cultural diversity, justice, law and order and interdependence.
- Know how democratic systems work and understand how individual citizens, public opinion, lobby groups, and the media can contribute and have an influence and impact. (KS4)
- Have a developing global awareness of contemporary issues and events including human rights and sustainable development. (KS4)

Emotional Aspect
- Know how to resolve conflict and negotiate agreement.

Spiritual Aspect
- Be aware of their character, strengths and weaknesses.
- Have insight into their beliefs and values in the context of those in society and propagated by the media.
- Know how their beliefs and values affect their identity and life style. (KS4)

Moral Aspect
- Recognise moral issues and dilemmas in life situations.
- Know what they believe to be right and wrong actions and understand the issues involved.
- Be aware of the factors involved in making moral judgements. (KS4)
- Identify a set of values and principles by which to live. (KS4)

Vocational Aspect
- Understand a range of economic and industrial issues related to their role as consumers and future providers and their responsibilities in personal finance. (KS4)

Northern Ireland

At key stage 4, students should be enabled to:
- respond to the specific challenges and opportunities which diversity and inclusion present in Northern Ireland and the wider world;
- identify and exercise their rights and social responsibilities in relation to local, national and global issues;
- develop their understanding of the role of society and government in safeguarding individual and collectives rights in order to promote equality and to ensure that everyone is treated fairly;
- develop their understanding how to participate in a range of democratic processes;
- develop awareness of key democratic institutions and their role in promoting inclusion, justice and democracy;
- develop awareness of the role of non-governmental organisations

This document will examine many of the issues related to Local and Global Citizenship and will attempt to exemplify the above statements (see Section 4).

Key concepts in Local and Global Citizenship Concept Interpretation Diversity and inclusion
Investigation of the concepts of diversity and inclusion provides opportunities for young people to consider the range and extent of diversity in societies locally and globally and to identify the challenges and opportunities which diversity and inclusion present. Investigating diversity in a local and global citizenship context is about encouraging young people to see the breadth of diversity in their own community and the challenges and opportunities that this may bring. Such an investigation would involve appropriate exploration of issues like gender, sexuality, ethnicity, religion, political beliefs etc., which would be in local, national and global

Equality and Social Justice
Investigation of the concepts of equality and justice provides opportunities for young people to understand that inequality and injustice exist; that they have an impact on individuals, groups and society; and that individuals, governments and society have responsibilities to promote equality and justice. Investigating Equality and Social Justice in a local and global citizenship context is about allowing young people opportunities to examine how inequalities can arise in society and how some people can experience inequality or discrimination on the basis of their group identity e.g. section 75 groups- racial group, disability, religious beliefs, gender etc. Furthermore investigating how some people are excluded from playing a full part in society as a result of their material circumstances will help young people engage with a range of social justice issues like homelessness, poverty and refugees.

Democracy and Active Participation
Investigation of the concepts of democracy and active participation provides opportunities for young people to understand how to participate in, and to influence democratic processes and to be aware of some key democratic institutions and their role in promoting inclusion, justice and democracy.

Human Rights and Social Responsibility is the core theme of local and global citizenship. Young people should be provided with opportunities to understand that a globally accepted values-base exists, within the various human rights international charters, which outline the rights and responsibilities of individuals and groups in democratic societies.

Rights and values will clash in any society. Young people should consider how to handle these conflicts through democratic processes. It then becomes important to consider how, in a diverse society which aspires to be just and equitable, individuals and groups can influence the decision making process.

Teachers' Notes: Addressing Bullying at Classroom Level

This book is part of the Life Skills Series and aims to provide ideas and strategies for dealing with difficult situations that students must sometimes endure. There may be situations that arise within your classroom or school environment that need special consideration.

Examples include:

❑ A student may be the victim of bullying at school or at home;
❑ A student may be displaying bullying behaviour;
❑ Students may be depressed or suicidal;
❑ Students may be the victim of physical or emotional abuse.

Part of the approach of this book involves providing realistic "scenarios" for some of the issues outlined above, as a basis for promoting discussion and learning opportunities specific to the problem. Many of these issues are of a sensitive nature, and while some of the scenarios may be particularly relevant to individual class members, other students may be exposed to such issues for the first time.

The issues raised in the role-play cards and activities are designed to promote whole class discussion on such issues based on students' individual experiences. The sheets are also ideal as homework activities for students to complete in their own time. Where possible, encourage students to discuss the sheets with their parents/guardians. Students can later reflect on their ideas and thoughts as a whole class or in small groups.

It is intended that these sheets be used at the teacher's discretion and/or in conjunction with counselling from qualified school counsellors and support staff. The activities are designed to facilitate discussion and to promote a friendly and open classroom climate for exchanging thoughts and ideas. The main aim of the sheets is to allow students to see that their reactions to certain events are normal and that bullying behaviours are not acceptable.

Bullying Defined

Most people have a vision in their heads about bullies. They usually picture a larger person who likes to throw their weight around by picking fights with other kids. This person may steal other students' food or equipment, or threaten violence. However, bullies come in all shapes and sizes from the tall boy in Year Seven right down to the tiny blonde Year One princess.

The act of bullying itself can take many forms. Bullies do not have to use physical violence in order for an act to be deemed as bullying. Bullying can be verbal, social, psychological and/or physical.

There are also a number of types of victims. Some personality types are more prone to bullying than other students.

Three examples of common bullying scenarios:

❑ A group of children are happily playing when a girl arrives on the scene. As the girl gets closer, the other students turn their backs and whisper among themselves making it clear that the child is not welcome to join the game. As the girl moves on, the remaining students giggle and whisper behind her back.

❑ The school bus stops and a boy that needs to get off makes his way from the back seat to the front. As he does this, another student sticks out his foot on purpose, causing the boy to trip over. The other students laugh.

❑ Two girls are walking home and are discussing another classmate. One says, "I heard that she doesn't even know how to read yet." The other child says, "Really, well I heard she can't even count to 15."

Some facts about bullying:

❑ The main forms of bullying include teasing, humiliating, excluding, ignoring, physical assault, stealing from students and spreading rumours.

❑ Most acts of bullying are done for attention.

❑ Bullying can start at school and continue right throughout life.

❑ Bullying in the workplace is just as prevalent as it is in the playground.

❑ It is important that students are educated about the impact of bullying on victims and the implications of bullying for both the bullies and the victims in the long term.

For Teachers: Looking After Yourself

Some of the issues raised in the Life Skills Series, particularly bullying and conflict resolution, can seriously impact on the teacher who has to face such issues within a class or school environment. Situations described in the front of this book can take their toll on the classroom teacher in several forms. It is important that teachers remember to take some time out to process their own emotions and thoughts on the issues that can sometimes arise in their classroom.

Teachers in such positions may develop symptoms of stress. Some common reactions can include:

- ❑ Feelings of anger and frustration directed at students, parents and other staff members;
- ❑ Feeling of inadequacy regarding ability to cope with difficult situations;
- ❑ Feelings of guilt when a positive outcome is not achieved;
- ❑ Feelings of helplessness or depression that may cause insomnia, loss of appetite and loss of concentration.

After any critical incident, opportunities for debriefing and consulting with support staff should be given, to help prevent or minimise stress related symptoms.

It is important that teachers accept the things that they cannot change rather than trying to take responsibility for something they have no control over.

Useful Websites:

- **www.bbc.co.uk/health/conditions/.../emotion_stress.shtml** - Managing Stress
- **www.hse.gov.uk/stress/** - Work Related Stress
- **www.atl.org.uk/health-and-safety/stress/stress-management.asp**- stress management in the workplace
- **www.jweducation.com/childstress.ppt** - Child Stress (PowerPoint Presentation)

Notes: Practical Strategies for the Classroom

One of the main phrases teachers hear frequently while addressing actions of bullying, is to "promote a safe and caring classroom environment". While it is taken for granted that teachers strive to promote a cooperative and cohesive class, the question still remains about how teachers can achieve a "safe" environment in the practical sense.

Practical tips:

❑ Create a 'Bully-Bin' where intimidated students can anonymously leave notes for the teacher about bullying incidents.

❑ Hold regular class meetings where students can discuss what is happening in the playground.

❑ Ask students to design posters with anti-bullying slogans to be displayed around the classroom, library and canteen.

What to say to victims of bullying:

❑ Tell the victim to pretend not to hear hurtful comments.

❑ Use silent "self-talk" such as, "That's their problem, not mine", or, "I'm OK", to reinforce self-confidence.

❑ Encourage children to talk about their experiences. Strongly emphasise that reporting acts of bullying is not to be seen as "dobbing" or "telling tales".

❑ Devise ways that students can develop greater self-assertiveness. This is best done through meaningful activities such as role-play and drama. Building self confidence and assertiveness in students will better equip them to be able to face the bully without becoming scared, upset, abusive or violent.

Strategies for students who are bullied:
Tell the student:

❑ Walk away and ignore the bully. Most bullies are looking for a reaction, if you ignore their behaviour, they may get bored and will stop bothering you.

❑ Talk about your problem to the teacher as well as friends or parents. These people will aim to give you the support and counselling that you need. It is a good idea to speak about bullying acts in detail, especially if you think the bully may be bullying others.

❑ Be confident – use body language that shows you are not afraid. Easy to say and hard to do, but if you look scared, it will encourage the bully to continue with the bullying behaviour. Practise what you will say in front of a mirror.

❑ DO NOT ATTEMPT TO DEAL WITH THIS PROBLEM ALONE, YOU NEED ADULT SUPPORT. *THE PROBLEM IS NOT YOU.* IT IS THE BULLY WHO HAS THE PROBLEM.

❑ DO NOT EVER TRY TO DEAL WITH THE BULLY BY USING PHYSICAL FORCE. THIS WILL ONLY INCREASE THE PROBLEM.

❑ Bullies usually pick on kids who are by themselves. Try to stick with your group of friends.

❑ Learn to carry yourself with confidence. Bullies are usually on the look out for kids who are quiet and possibly awkward. Stand up straight and look that bully in the eye!

Many studies have shown that children who are bullied at school and in the community, often grow up to be adult victims of bullying. Use the strategies above to help break that bullying cycle!

Aber Education

Useful Resources for the Classroom

Literature for Students

Junior Primary

❑ Cannon, Janell (2000), *Crickwing*, Harcourt Publishing, Florida. USA. ISBN: 0152017909

❑ Casely, Judith (2001), *Bully*, Greenwillow Books, New York. USA. ISBN: 0688160921

❑ Lester, Helen (2002) *Hooway for Wadney Wat*, Houghton Mifflin Books, Boston. USA. ISBN: 061821612X

Middle Primary

❑ Mark, Jan (1999), *Lady Long-Legs*, Sprinter Series, Walker Books Ltd. United Kingdom. ISBN: 0744578345.

Upper Primary

❑ Koss, Amy (2002), *The Girls*, Puffin Books, Penguin, Australia. ISBN: 0142300330.

❑ Shusterman, Neal, (2002), *The Shadow Club*, Penguin Putnam Books for Young Readers, Penguin Group, USA. ISBN: 0142300942.

❑ Shusterman, Neal, (2002), *Shadow Club Rising*, Penguin Putnam Books for Young Readers, Penguin Group, USA. ISBN: 0525468358.

Teacher Resources

General Resources

❑ www.lifeskills4kids.com/ - *Life Skills* (lesson plans).

   ❑ www.teach-nology.com/ideas/bullying/ - A web portal for teachers. This site contains entries from teachers who have successfully implemented anti-bullying strategies in their classroom. A valuable resource to combat bullying behaviour.

❑ http://www.nspcc.org.uk/getinvolved/ raisemoney/fundraisinginschools/ defeatbullying/teaching_resources_wda50411. html On the day we visited there were five free lessons for teachers to use.

❑ http://www.bobsedulinks.com/teachers. htm, lots of links from Bob

❑ http://www.teachers.tv/bullying can't be sure it is still available but it was the day we looked and we were impressed.

❑ http://www.focusas.com/Bullying.html BULLYING What Parents and Teachers Should Know

Discipline Resources

▶ www.disciplinehelp.com/ - *Discipline Help*

This informative website contains a wealth of information for educators. It highlights 117 specific misbehaviours that occur in the classroom. The behaviours are grouped into four main motivations for misbehaviour:

   ❑ revenge

   ❑ power

   ❑ self-confidence

   ❑ attention seeking

❑ teacher2b.com/discipline/bullies.htm *Dealing with Classroom Bullies.* Provides information on strategies.

❑ www.schoolskills.com/ - *Terrific Teacher Tool Kit.* This is a very handy resource with sections titles including "32 Mistakes Most Teachers Make and Want to Avoid!" and "Your Classroom – 67 Ways to Improve It!"

❑ www.primaryteachers.org/ *Primary Teachers' Nook.* Contains lesson plan ideas, thematic units and information about classroom discipline.

❑ www.theteachersguide.com/ ClassManagement.htm - *Classroom Management.* Extensive website with sections and articles on discipline and strategies.

🖱 Websites for Students

Families, Friends and Feelings

❑ **The Anti-bullying network** Set up in Scotland and therefore school references are Scottish eg Highers, stuffed full of info. www.antibullying. net/

❑ **BULLYING 42EXPLORE**

Basic information for students on bullying plus links, webquests and activities. Excellent www.42explore2.com/bully.htm

❑ **STOP BULLYING NOW**

Excellent US site, Good information including What Bullying Is, What You Can Do, Cool Stuff, and What Adults Can Do. The Cool Stuff section has animated webisodes on bullying along with 8 games. Appropriate for elementary/middle school students. /www.stopbullyingnow.hrsa.gov/index asp?area=main

❑ **BBC** site on school issues, includes details on bullying. Excellent as ever from the BBC. On the day we checked there was great advice from an NSPCC advisor

www.bbc.co.uk/schools/studentlife/ schoolissues/

❑ **Anti-Bullying Alliance:** Excellent site if a little formal looking. Lots of stuff and there is a young anti-bullying alliance

www.anti-bullyingalliance.org.uk

❑ **Antibullying week**: The site was a little dated when we looked at it but there was good stuff on it. www.antibullyingweek.co.uk

❑ **Childline** excellent site and excellent organisation www.childline.org.uk Freephone 0800 1111,

❑ **Kidscape:** Their website says they are committed to keeping children safe from abuse 020 7730 3300 www.kidscape.org.uk

❑ **Beatbullying**, on their site they say 'Founded in 1999, multi award-winning Beatbullying empowers young people to lead anti-bullying campaigns in their schools and local communities' www.beatbullying.org.

❑ **Bullying UK** On their website they say 'Bullying UK is the new name for the award winning charity Bullying Online which was founded in 1999 by journalist Liz Carnell from Harrogate and her son John, as a direct result of their experience of dealing with school bullying, which included taking successful legal action against an education authority. The UK's leading anti-bullying charity In the last eight years the charity's website has become the number one resource for people using search engines like Google, MSN and Yahoo to find reliable information on a variety of bullying issues' **www.bullying.co.uk**

❑ **Anti-Bullying** events for young people by young people. Strategies to tackle the bully, bullies and bullying. Anti-Bullying Strategies, Solutions and Events. www.bully.org/

❑ **Cyber bullying**: This is more and more of a problem for young people and this site does help. It is a Canadian site www.cyberbullying. org

❑ **Being Bullied by a Teacher** - Teen Issues (UK) it should not happen but it does. This site has some info but also a lot of ads www.teenissues.co.uk/BeingBulliedByATeacher.html

❑ **Menstuff**, not the best of titles for a website but this site has lots of info for young people. It is an American site so notice the different way they write dates www.menstuff.org/issues/byissue/bullying.html

Websites for Teachers and Parents

- *No Bully*. This site from New Zealand contains definitions, strategies, resources and information about how to control bullying and how to promote bully-free environments at school and in the community **www.nobully. org.nz**.

- *National Coalition Against Bullying.* An Australian site, This innovative initiative brings together a group of individuals from key organisations with the aim of raising awareness of bullying issues and bringing about social change in the community. The site contains an extensive resource list as well as an excellent question and answer section www.ncab.org.au.

- The *Bullying - No Way! Project* - was developed and is managed by all participating Australian education authorities in State and Territory government education systems as well as the National Catholic Education Commission, the National Council of Independent Schools' Associations and the Commonwealth Department of Education, Science and Training. The website includes discussion boards, forums, resource lists, sections for parents, teachers and students, ideas for the classroom, information about legislation, online activities for students and much more! **www.bullyingnoway.com.au**

- They say: **Bullying.org's** purpose is to eliminate bullying in our society by supporting individuals and organizations to take positive actions against bullying through the sharing of resources, and to guide and champion them in creating non-violent solutions to the challenges and problems associated with bullying. www. bullying.org

- **NSPCC,** they say: We want to help stamp out bullying at school. Everyone - children, teachers, adults - can help put a stop to child bullying.

Every school should have a strong anti-bullying policy. Everyone who wants to stop bullying at school should have someone they can turn to for help. There are lots of reasons why some people start bullying, and why others are bullied. There is something about all of us that others might pick on, but bullying, at school or outside school, is always wrong, no matter what. www.nspcc.org.uk

- **Direct gov:** advice for parents www.direct.gov.uk/ en/Parents/

- **Tooter4 kids**: Packed full of kid friendly advice, you need to make this available for your children/ students /www.tooter4kids.com

- **Kids against bullying**, an excellent child friendly site, US based.

  www.pacerkidsagainstbullying.org

- **Beyond Bullying**: website from Leicestershire Ed Psych service, three themes, 1. Improving Behaviour 2. Developing inclusive practice 3. REDUCING BULLYING

  www.beyondbullying.com

- **Bully beware** Canadian site that sells a number of products www.bullybeware.com

- **Dr Ken Rigby** researcher who provides a lot of informed information and is worthy of your time to read what he has to say. Makes a point that much on the internet is actually uninformed opinion, this is worth remembering.Also provides a number of links www.kenrigby.net

- **Bully Free Zone** on the day we visited they had a free download on cyber bullying www. bullyfreezone.co.uk

Activity 1 — Bursting the Bully Bubble (1)

Teachers' Notes:

Photocopy and cut out each of the scenarios below and on the following page. This activity can be done in small groups, pairs or as an individual activity. The Reflection sheet on Page 18 is designed to facilitate discussion among class members. Distribute a "Reflection" sheet for students to complete for EACH story.

City Slickers

Aaron has just moved from a country town up to the "big smoke". He is starting to enjoy going to the new school but is terrified of the bus trip home as there is a gang of boys who have started to pick on him. One of the boys, Jake, is in Aaron's class at school and never seems to cause any trouble during class time. However, Jake links up with his older brother Brad and his mates when it is time to catch the bus home. The boys have been teasing Aaron about being from the country and push him around when he tries to get on the bus. On one occasion, Jake threw Aaron's school bag out of the bus when the doors opened to let students out. Aaron was forced to get out at the wrong stop and had to walk twice as far to his house. Aaron has noticed that Jake doesn't have many friends in their class at school.

Texting Tactics

On Fiona's twelfth birthday, her parents bought her a mobile phone. Fiona didn't tell anyone what the number was or that she even had a phone and has been using the phone to bully other kids in her class and in the class below. She keeps sending anonymous text messages to other students saying that she is going to beat them up if they don't watch out. Sometimes, Fiona hears the kids talking about the text messages and she teases the students saying that they better be careful as someone is out to get them.

A Weighty Worry

Lucy is often picked on by other girls in her class as she doesn't seem to be able to keep up with the latest fads and fashion. Some girls even comment on Lucy's weight, saying that she needs to buy new clothes as she is bursting out of her old ones. Lucy is very upset by the teasing and has stopped eating. She also thinks she can save up some of her lunch money by not eating, which will allow her to buy some of the cool clothes.

Netball Nasties

Clara plays netball on the weekends with some girls from her town. The girls go to another school in the town and are often teasing Clara about how uncool her school is as it is not a state school. When they are on the court, the girls refuse to throw the ball to Clara and then complain when their team loses, saying that it was Clara's fault. The girls try to push Clara over whenever they can and have told her that she is a loser and she doesn't belong in their team. Clara loves playing netball but is starting to think of quitting as she is dreading the Saturday games.

Activity 2

Bursting the Bully Bubble (2)

Brainy Bother

Simon had always been a clever student and was proud of his school record. When he moved to his new school, he was always the first to answer any questions that the teacher asked the class and always did extremely well in tests. After a week, three boys in Simon's class started teasing him at break time, saying that he was the teacher's pet and a complete nerd. They imitated him answering questions in class and some of the other kids would laugh when they saw Simon being picked on. Simon started to stop answering as many questions and also started to deliberately get poor marks in some of the tests. At his old school, the other students had looked up to him, but at the new school, he found out that it was very uncool to be clever. After a while, the teacher asked Simon if anything was bothering him as his school work was slipping. Simon just shrugged and said, "I am just not that smart!"

Footy Monsters

Matthew is being bullied by a number of boys in his football team. Each time he returns to the change rooms after a game, someone has done something with his bag. One day Matthew found his school jumper in a toilet bowl and another time his bag was filled with mud from the other boys' footy boots. When Matthew misses a tackle or goal, the boys tease him about it the next day at school, telling him he let the whole school down.

Lunch Loner

Alex isn't very popular in his class and doesn't have many friends. No one pays much attention to him and the teacher hardly seems to notice him. Alex has started teasing younger kids on his bus. He has told them that he and his "mates" will beat them up at break if they don't hand over their lunch money to him. Because he has no friends of his own, Alex seeks out the kids during break and lunch times and says that he will go and get his "mates" if they don't share their snacks with him.

Home-work Heavy

Jack is the captain of the junior cricket team and is fairly popular at school. However, he is struggling with his schoolwork and is often unable to complete his homework. In class he sits next to David. He has been threatening David by telling him he will be dropped from the team if he doesn't take home Jack's homework. David is not very good at sport but doesn't want to be dropped from the team. Jack has also threatened to get his older brother to beat David up if he does not do what he says.

Activity 3 — Reflection: Bully Bubbles

👉 Use this page to reflect about the issues in each story on Pages 16-17.

Name of story: ▶

1 Who are the people involved in this story?

_____

_____

_____

2 What is the bullying behaviour?

_____

_____

_____

3 Why is the bullying occurring?

_____

_____

_____

4 What are the options that the bullied person has?

_____

_____

_____

Bully Bubbles

5 What would you do if you were the bully's victim in the story?

_____

_____

_____

6 Have you ever been involved in some way (either as a bully, onlooker or victim) in a story like this one?

_____

_____

_____

Reflect on the situation by chatting about your responses to a class mate.

Aber Education

Activity 4

Who is a Bully?

 Think back to some of the bullying tactics mentioned in the stories on pages 16 and 17.

Make a list of all the things that bullies might do.

- _____
- _____
- _____
- _____
- _____
- _____
- _____
- _____

❶ Have any of these "acts of bullying" ever happened to you? Describe.

_____
_____
_____
_____
_____

❷ Spot the bully in this line-up. Circle him/her.

Why did you pick this person?

_____
_____

❸ Why do you think bullies behave the way they do?

_____
_____
_____
_____
_____

❹

What can you say about the bullies that you know? Think of some words that you could use to describe their behaviour.

_____
_____
_____
_____
_____

B – Bad

U – Unkind

L – Lying

L – Lazy

Y – Yelling

Activity 5 | Profile of a Bully

Draw a bully in the box below. Remember bullies don't walk around the place with a t-shirt saying, "Bully of the Year!".

- **Write down some of the things that make this person a bully.**
- **Write these things in different colours around your drawing.**

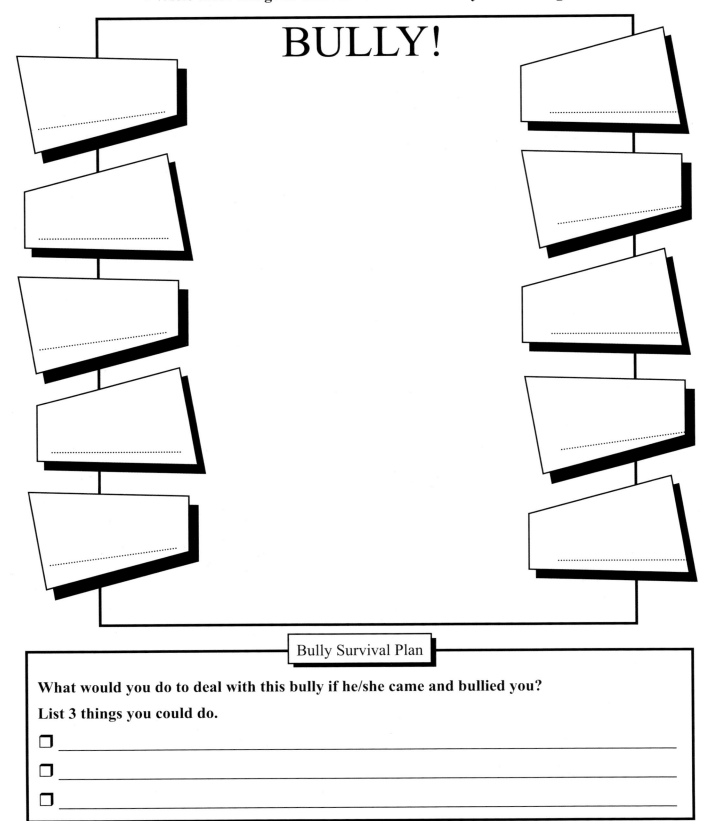

BULLY!

Bully Survival Plan

What would you do to deal with this bully if he/she came and bullied you?

List 3 things you could do.

☐ _____

☐ _____

☐ _____

Aber Education

Activity 6 | # Bully Checklist

☞ ☐ Are you being bullied? ☐ Are you a bully? ☐ Is your best friend a bully?

Tick the square in each box if you think it is showing bullying behaviour.

How many boxes did you tick? _____

Have you ever been involved in a story like any of the scenes in the boxes? Discuss these pictures with your classmates.

Activity 7

Comic Strip Bully

In the boxes below, create a comic strip that shows a bully in action. Make sure you use speech bubbles to show what is being said in each scene. You may like to think of a real life bully situation that you may have been involved in.

Now draw another scene to demonstrate how this bullying problem could be resolved.

Aber Education

Activity 8   What Happens in My School?

Read the statements below and then answer them according to how you feel. Tick the boxes to show your answer.

	Always	Sometimes	Never
1. I have been bullied at school.	☐	☐	☐
2. I have been taught things to say and do if I am bullied.	☐	☐	☐
3. Our class has a set of rules that we helped to develop.	☐	☐	☐
4. I am happy at school.	☐	☐	☐
5. Bullying occurs at my school.	☐	☐	☐
6. When bullying occurs, it means a school rule has been broken.	☐	☐	☐
7. I tell the teachers if bullying occurs.	☐	☐	☐
8. I feel comfortable talking about bullying behaviour with teachers.	☐	☐	☐
9. I have been shown helpful ways to deal with bullying.	☐	☐	☐
10. My school is interested in finding out what kids think about bullying	☐	☐	☐
11. I have seen other kids being bullied at school.	☐	☐	☐
12. I have stayed away from school when scared of being bullied.	☐	☐	☐
13. I talk to my parents about bullying.	☐	☐	☐
14. In the past, I have been a bully to other children.	☐	☐	☐
15. Sometimes I feel afraid while walking home from school.	☐	☐	☐

Discuss your responses with a partner.

Teachers' Notes: Group Work

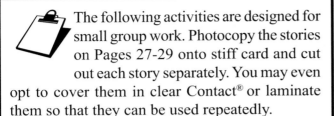 The following activities are designed for small group work. Photocopy the stories on Pages 27-29 onto stiff card and cut out each story separately. You may even opt to cover them in clear Contact® or laminate them so that they can be used repeatedly.

The aims of this activity are to allow students to understand that individuals have differing perceptions about bullying behaviour, and to identify how best to address such situations.

Instructions

Divide the class into small groups of 4-5 students. Do this by numbering each child and then telling them to move into groups of their particular number. In this way, the groups are random and students will be encouraged to express their feelings on bullying to students from out of their immediate comfort zone.

Each group needs to nominate a reader, a scribe and a speaker. Alternatively, these roles can be rotated. The reader will read the card to the other members while the scribe will note down all of the group's responses and solutions to the situation described on the card. The speaker will then stand up and report on the group's main ideas to the rest of the class. Elect a timekeeper for the class and give this student a five-minute timer. (A stopwatch is ideal, as they will need to keep time for five and two minute intervals).

❶ In groups, students dissect the bullying story on the card.

❷ Students rate the situation according to how serious they see the problem.

❸ The group then brainstorms actions they could take after reading the questions on the board as specified in the next column.

❹ Each group should suggest a number of options for dealing with this behaviour.

❺ After five minutes, the timekeeper calls "Time". Each group then has two minutes to vote on the option they think is best for that particular situation.

❻ The speakers take turns to address the entire class. They should clearly explain their group's findings and disclose the "level of seriousness" rating they gave the situation.

❼ Alternatively, this activity can be done individually. Photocopy the Conflict Resolution sheets on Pages 25 and 26. Students/groups will need one sheet for each story.

Write these questions on the board:

❶ Is this bullying behaviour?

❷ What are the options for dealing with this behaviour?

❸ What is the best option? (i.e. a win-win outcome)

Role-Play Activities

In groups, allow the students to role-play the activities using the win-win solutions that they suggested. After each role-play, facilitate a discussion about the outcome and whether this tactic would work in a real life situation.

Opinions (Page 30)

Students can use this page to provide their opinions on the levels of seriousness of each story. Allow time for the children to discuss their views and reflect on each story (in small groups). Regroup as a whole class and discuss. If time, you might like to allow each student to speak, otherwise each group could nominate a speaker.

Conflict Resolution - Looking at the Options

How to Solve a Problem

Before you can come to any kind of positive solution, you need to look carefully at the problem. This will lead you to make some choices on how best to deal with this situation. This strategy can be applied to any of the situations on the role-play cards.

For example, if two older children are bullying you in the playground, you have a few options. You could:

❑ run away from them;

❑ tell the teacher about them;

❑ try and defend yourself or;

❑ do something mean to these kids when they are not looking – like steal their lunch!

However, if you look at each of these options, you will find that there are positives and negatives that could occur.

Let's say you go with the first option and run away.

A positive aspect could be listed as:

❑ **You have removed yourself from the threat of danger.**

A negative aspect could include:

❑ **You have given the bullies what they want – to see you scared!**

Let's say you go with the last option.

You may choose to get revenge on these students in another way, for example, by putting sand in their lunchbox, or putting snails in their back pack when they are not looking!

A positive aspect for you might be:

❑ **It would make you feel good to see them angry.**

A negative aspect would include:

❑ **Making the bully even more determined to make your life a misery.**

THINK ABOUT ...

What is a way that you could deal with this situation and end up with a positive outcome for all involved? This would be known as a **WIN-WIN** situation. Explain your WIN-WIN tactic below.

_____

_____

_____

_____

_____

_____

_____

_____

_____

ROLE-PLAYS & STRATEGIES •

Activity 9 | Conflict Resolution - Time To Sort it Out!

Use this worksheet to help you better understand the stories on the cards.

❶ What is the actual problem?

_____

_____

_____

_____

_____

❷ How serious do you think this problem is? Give your reasons.

_____

_____

_____

_____

❸ Give the problem a rating out of 10.
(**1** means "not very serious" and **10** means "extremely serious").

❹ List all the options available for the people involved. Consider the consequences of each action.

_____

_____

_____

_____

_____

_____

❺ Out of your choices above, work out which one is the best solution.

Read over what you have written, put a ☐ next to the negative aspects of this action and a ☐ next to the positive outcomes. The best solution will mean a positive result. Write your final choice below.

_____

_____

❻ Group Activity: Role-play the story using your solution.

Keeping it Real!

❑ How well do you think you resolved this issue?

_____

_____

_____

_____

_____

❑ Do you think this action would actually work in a real life situation? Explain your thoughts.

_____

_____

_____

What did other students in your group think about this role-play?

_____

_____

Activity 10 Role-Play Cards: Bully Tactics! (1)

Story 1

While playing on the basketball court with two friends, you were approached by some of the older kids who want to play a game of basketball with two teams. They asked if your friends would play on their team. You asked which team you were going to be on and one of the girls laughed and said that you weren't good enough to be in the team and that you may as well go and find something else to do!

Story 3

Sandra was walking home from school one day when she heard Caroline, a prefect, start teasing Joseph, one of the younger children who was walking in front of her. Sandra couldn't believe what she was hearing. Joseph was upset and turned around to tell Caroline to stop teasing him and then Caroline started swearing at him. The younger children then ran away and Sandra saw that they were crying. As they ran away, Caroline started throwing stones at them. Caroline was one of the head prefects at school as well as the sports captain. It seemed strange for her to behave like that, as she looked friendly during school assemblies.

Sandra then saw Caroline turn to her friend, saying, "No one will believe them, after all, we are prefects!"

Story 2

Joel, a boy in your class, is playing on the tennis court at morning play with some of his friends. Another boy, Rex, wants to join in but Joel says to you that he is useless at hitting the ball. Then, Joel starts hitting the ball very hard in Rex's direction. You are sure some of the shots are directed straight at Rex. Rex gets upset and the others laugh.

Story 4

You are playing handball at break with some of your friends. Simone, a girl from another class, and some of her friends line up to play. Simone deliberately gets you out when it is her turn and laughs. You get angry and throw the ball at her when she is not looking and she falls over. Simone then runs over to the teacher with her friends and they all say that you threw the ball at her for no reason.

Activity 11 Role-Play Cards: Bully Tactics! (2)

Story 5

Katrina is thirteen and is the school swimming captain. Two of the girls in Katrina's class at school are jealous of her success at swimming and have started spreading rumours that Katrina has been shoplifting from the school canteen. They have also started telling certain students that she has been copying off other students' work during class.

Story 7

Simon is in a split class at school and not very popular with the kids in his class. He seems to enjoy teasing a couple of boys in the year level below. He puts them down in front of other students and often scribbles on their work that is displayed around the classroom. He writes nasty comments next to their names and seems to do this only for a reaction from other students.

Story 6

Kelly is new to the school and has not had time to make new friends as she is training for the county gymnastics trials. During maths, Kelly answers all of the teacher's questions correctly and the teacher is pleased. Another student, Gabrielle, is getting tired of Kelly being a know-it-all. She pulls Kelly's hair when they are sitting on the mat. Kelly turns around but doesn't know who did it. Later that day, Gabrielle imitates the teacher praising Kelly as Kelly walks past.

Story 8

Miranda is in Year 9 and lately she and her friends have been demanding that some of the Year 7 children hand over their lunch money. Miranda tells them that she will get her older sister and her high school mates to bash them up after school if they don't pay. She also said that if they tell the teacher about it they would be asking for trouble. Miranda warned the younger children that she knows where they all live and she will come around to their house with her mates.

Activity 12   Role-Play Cards: Bully Tactics! (3)

Story 11

Alex is in Year 7 and is not doing very well at school. He has noticed that someone has written nasty things about him on the backs of the toilet doors. He thinks that it is Peter, a boy in his class. Peter has been spreading stories about Alex and says that Alex still wets the bed, which isn't true.

Story 13

Leon is in Year 7 and has managed to annoy all of his friends by telling lies. No one wants to play with him during school play times or on the weekends. He has got his big bully brother Bradley to help him make new friends. Bradley, who is in year 10 has told some of the boys that they better play with Leon otherwise he will get his "gang" onto them.

Story 12

Samantha is in Year 7 and sits in a group with Carrie and Charlotte during class. She has started copying the girls' work and has been using their ideas when the teacher asks questions during lessons. She has also started stealing their markers and pencils. Samantha has warned the girls that if they tell on her, she will get her dad involved. Samantha's dad is the town policeman and the girls are very scared of him.

Story 14

Violet is new to her school and has had trouble making friends with the girls in her class. She has started bullying two of the younger girls at the school. She has told them that they have to play with her at lunchtime in the playground. Violet makes up the rules as she goes along and tells the two girls that they are silly. The girls are too scared to say anything to Violet as she is a lot bigger than them and is really mean.

Story 15

Evan lives next door to Samuel and they both attend the same school. Samuel's parents are from another country. Evan thinks that they are too different to live in his street, as they don't speak English very well. Evan tells all of the other kids in the class that Samuel's family are weird. He even makes up stories about what goes on and tells the other kids who laugh.

Activity 13 | Opinion Time - Bully Tactics

☞ Think back to the role-play cards. There were 13 stories altogether.

Which story did you think was the most serious?

Explain in detail the reasons for your choice.

Story #

- _____
- _____
- _____
- _____
- _____
- _____

Now decide which story was the least worrying:

Again, give reasons for your choice.

Story #

- _____
- _____
- _____
- _____
- _____
- _____

In groups of four, compare your answers.

Did most people have the same opinions as you? Write down some interesting points that came out of your discussion.

_____

_____

_____

_____

Aber Education

Double Vision

Activity 14

Jacob is a fairly popular boy at school but struggles with his school work. He is very good at sport and has acted as a school captain at interschool sports day. He has a group of friends who look up to him as a role model and leader on the sporting field.

However, in class Jacob seems to enjoy teasing a couple of other boys while they are working. The boys he teases are not very interested in sport, preferring to spend their spare time on the computers. Jacob calls them names and often writes hurtful comments next to their names on class charts displayed around the room. He will often walk over to where they are working and scribble on their work. He always calls them losers and says that guys like that are a "waste of space". Jacob's friends think this is funny and the teacher has noticed that Jacob only seems to behave like this in front of his friends. Jacob never bothers anyone during sport times.

Step into a Bully's Shoes!

Imagine you are Jacob. Re-read the story above and discuss the problem as you see it, putting yourself in Jacob's shoes. Include your feelings and possible actions that should be taken.

_____
_____
_____
_____
_____
_____
_____
_____
_____
_____

Now pretend you are one of the boys that has been teased by Jacob.

Write your version of the story. Include your feelings and possible actions that should be taken.

_____
_____
_____
_____
_____
_____
_____
_____

Activity 15 — Bully Poems

Have a go at writing some funny poems.
Write a short poem from a bully's point of view.

_____

_____

_____

_____

_____

_____

_____

_____

_____

_____

_____

_____

Here's an acrostic poem that has a warning to bullies. Write one of your own.

B – *Bullies aren't cool,*
U – *Ugly scenes at school,*
L – *Lying and telling tales,*
L – *Laughing when a kid fails,*
Y – *Yelling nasty words:*
I – *"Idiots!" "Losers!" "Nerds!"*
N – *Nasty names can hurt,*
G – *Go away bullies! We're on alert!*

B – _____
U – _____
L – _____
L – _____
Y – _____
I – _____
N – _____
G – _____

A Limerick for a Bully!

Finish the limerick below. Make sure your poem has a positive message. Choose a starting line below or think of one of your own!

Remember: There are only five lines in a limerick. The first, second and fifth lines rhyme with each other. The third and fourth lines rhyme with each other as well.

> **A bully once terrorised a school,**
> **After a while he looked like a fool,**
> **The kids told him "NO!"**
> **"Be nice or just go!"**
> **And the bully realised he was uncool.**

Limerick Starters

- There once was a bully at school ...

- A bully was hiding in the shed ...

- There was a young bully from town ...

_____

_____

_____

_____

_____

_____

_____

_____

Aber Education

Activity 16

Match Ups

Match the sentence beginnings with the sentence endings.

a. Being a bully ...   to spread stories about you.

b. Bullies like to receive ...   attention.

c. If you are bullied ...   people and leave them out.

d. Bullies are ...   for other people's things.

e. Bullies can be difficult ...   your lunch money or homework!

f. Sometimes bullies ignore ...   to pick out of a crowd.

g. Bullies have no respect ...   around us all the time.

h. Bullies think it's funny ...   is not cool at all.

i. A bully might try and steal ...   you should talk to your teacher.

j. Think carefully about what you ...   would say to a bully.

Listen Up!

Think of a bully that you have seen in action. Think carefully and then write down what you might say if bullied by this person.

Share your work with the person that sits next to you.

_____

_____

_____

_____

_____

_____

_____

_____

Remember:

If you are bullied by anyone, write it down somewhere and write down all the times it happens.
Discuss the bullying behaviour with your teacher or parents.

Activity 17 | A Letter For a Bully

 Sometimes it is easier to explain things to someone by writing your ideas down. Sometimes when we are angry about something we get all confused about what we really want to say.

Imagine you are being bullied either in class, in the playground, on the sports field or even at the shopping centre. Write a letter to the bully explaining how he/she annoys you sometimes. This letter is to help you clarify your thoughts about what is happening to you.

In your letter, include what you think the bully should do and say instead.

Dear Bully,

_____

_____

_____

_____

_____

_____

_____

_____

_____

_____

_____

_____

Aber Education

Teachers' Notes: Dealing with Problems

Periodically, situations arise that can cause conflict either at school, at home, in the playground or at weekend team events. Such situations might include bullying, teasing, aggression in sports or classroom activities, suspected child-abuse/neglect cases, times of grief, suicide prevention, and caring for yourself as a teacher through these events.

A problem solving approach is the best way to tackle such situations, especially where students are struggling with resolving the problem/s on their own. The process outlined below is ideally suited to these situations. For such problems, encourage students and/or parents and other teachers to work through and answer the following questions.

What is the problem?

❑ Who is involved?

❑ What is the issue?

❑ What resources might you need to solve this problem?

❑ Who do you need to speak to in order to solve the problem?

What are your options?

❑ What are the available options?

❑ What are the consequences of each option?

❑ What options do you think will work?

❑ What options might make the matter worse?

❑ What factors will influence your choice? (E.g. cost, feasibility, availability of resources and so on.)

What do you hope to achieve?

❑ What might happen in the short-term as a result of your choice of action?

❑ What might happen in the long-term as a result of your choice of action?

How are you going to carry out your action?

❑ What are the steps involved?

❑ Who will you need to involve?

❑ Do you need to practise this plan of action?

❑ How will you keep a positive attitude throughout this problem solving task?

REFLECTION

❑ What worked?

❑ What didn't work?

❑ What results were achieved?

❑ How can you modify your approach next time?

Dealing with Difficult Issues

Often students are unsure about what they are trying to achieve. Students may also have trouble communicating their ideas and thoughts in a clear manner. Many students are often misunderstood because the students themselves are unsure about what they believe should happen regarding a particular matter. Some students will believe there is nothing wrong, others may believe that the teacher is against them, and at other times students may be torn between what their parents are telling them and what their teachers are telling them.

How To Solve a Problem

☞ Use the boxes below to help you clarify the problem and sort out some options available.

What is the problem?

❏ Who is involved? ❏ What is the issue?
❏ What might I need to help solve this problem? ❏ Who can I speak to?

What do I hope to achieve?

❏ As a result of my actions, what will happen in the short-term?
❏ What will happen in the long-term?

How can I carry out the actions?

❏ What are the steps involved?
❏ Who is involved?

What are my options?

❏ What are the consequences for each option?
❏ What might work?
❏ What might make things worse?

REFLECTION

❏ What worked?

❏ What didn't work?

❏ What results were achieved?

❏ Did I achieve the right result?

❏ How can you modify your approach next time?

Aber Education

Teachers' Notes: Using a Problem Solving Approach

On the following pages are photocopiable "problem scenarios". Some of these situations may be directly relevant to students in your class. The problems touch on a range of social, moral and ethical issues some students may be facing. They include:

- Domestic violence
- Drug abuse
- Dangerous practices
- Emotional abuse
- Criminal activity
- Suicidal thoughts
- Family conflict
- Peer conflict
- Sexual issues
- Peer pressure
- Bullying
- Anger management

These scenarios are best used in an upper classroom as a lead-in to becoming a teenager and heading towards high school. Some of these cards may not be applicable to your class so please think carefully about the cards that you choose to use. These cards can also be completed as homework activities for individual students.

How to use these cards

Photocopy the cards and laminate or cover with clear Contact®.

Divide the class into small groups of 3-4 students. You may even like to plan this lesson as a partner activity. One student from each group selects a card for his/her group. Another student in the group is assigned the task of writing down students' ideas and reactions on a sheet of A4 paper. It is up to you as to how you want to run the activity but you can choose for all groups to be exploring the same scenario or each group can look at a different scenario each week. At the end of the lesson there should be an opportunity for group sharing, which is best done with all students sitting in a circle. No students should be forced to speak about anything, instead, encourage a friendly open discussion that invites students to express their feelings at their own discretion. Depending on the nature of your class, you may wish to keep the discussion activity within the small group situation rather than as a whole class, bearing in mind that vulnerable students may feel intimidated and less likely to contribute while in a larger group.

Individual Problems

On Page 43, an opportunity is given for students to discuss any problems they may be facing. The idea is to allow students to talk about issues that may be affecting them in daily life. Students should not feel compelled to discuss their problems and opportunities should be provided for sharing, only after having gained the trust from other group members. The group can then tackle students' individual situations using the problem solving approach. Importantly, this session should be carefully monitored by the teacher.

Reporting

Students should be able to obtain a copy of their group's reporting. Carefully read some of the responses from individual group members, bearing in mind that serious matters should be referred on to the school support service staff.

Discussion

These moral dilemmas and realistic scenarios are designed to provoke further discussions in this area, either about real life scenarios or how students have faced similar situations.

REFLECTION

The student reflection sheet on Page 44 can be completed as an individual activity after the group work sessions. This sheet provides opportunities for the student to express feelings that he/she may have been reluctant to share orally with group members.

Activity 18

Discussion Cards (a)

☞ Scenario 1

Michael's older brother Steven is 16. In the last few months, Steven has started acting very strangely at home and spends a lot of time in his room. When their parents are out, Michael often smells strange smoking odours coming out of Steven's room. He notices that Steven seems to just sit around a lot and has lost all interest in football and even girls. Whenever Michael tries to go and see Steven in his room, he is told to go away. Michael doesn't know Steven's room even looks like anymore as no one is allowed in there.

Steven has started asking Michael to lend him his pocket money. He said he will pay him back but he won't tell Michael what he needs it for. He has told Michael he will punch his lights out if he tells Mum or Dad.

☞ FOCUS QUESTIONS:

❶ **What do you think could be going on with Steven?**

❷ **If you were Michael, what would you say to Steven?**

❸ **What would you say to your parents?**

❹ **How could you help this situation?**

❺ **What could be a positive outcome in this situation**

☞ Scenario 2

Jarrad is in your year at school. He has never been interested in sport and is more often found in the library or on the computer when it comes to play time. Jarrad is quite popular in class, however, his closest friends are girls as the boys are mostly too embarrassed to be seen talking with him. He spends a lot of time talking to the girls and is interested in the same music. Jarrad has started wearing his hair in different styles and students in your class – and in other classes at your school – are starting to pick on Jarrad for being "different". They imitate his movements and call him names. They laugh when he answers questions in class and always turn his comments around to mean something rude. Jarrad pretends not to hear the cruel remarks and knows that the girls he is friends with are starting to feel that they might be picked on for being his friend.

☞ FOCUS QUESTIONS:

❶ **What do you think is going on with Jarrad?**

❷ **How would you treat Jarrad if he was in your class?**

❸ **Do you know anyone like Jarrad? Discuss?**

❹ **If you were one of Jarrad's friends what would you do?**

❺ **How could you help this situation?**

❻ **What could be a positive outcome in this situation?**

Aber Education

Activity 19

Discussion Cards (b)

☞ Scenario 3

Kelly is in Year 9 at the local high school. She plays netball in your Saturday game and all of the girls look up to her. You are in Year 7 and think that Kelly is pretty cool. One afternoon after netball, Kelly asks you if you want to go and hang out at the shops. Your mum lets you go and even gives you some pocket money to spend. On the way to the shopping centre, Kelly takes a packet of cigarettes out of her bag. Her older sister had bought them for her. Kelly lights up and asks if you want one. You don't know any students that smoke but you want Kelly to think you are cool.

☞ FOCUS QUESTIONS:

❶ **What would your choice be?**

❷ **What will you say to Kelly?**

☞ Scenario 4

Joanne is in your class at school but doesn't have many friends. She spends a lot of time playing basketball, usually just practising goal shooting by herself. You aren't close friends with her but you spend time with her after school as she goes home on the same school bus. Joanne's parents are going through a divorce and it has been very hard going on Joanne. She said that she never quite knows what she is in for when she arrives home each day. Joanne is sick of everything going on at home and there is no one she feels she can talk to about her family. One day Joanne tells you that she is thinking of running away.

☞ FOCUS QUESTIONS:

❶ **What do you say to Joanne?**

❷ **How could you help this situation?**

❸ **What could you change at school to help Joanne?**

❹ **What could you do if you were in Joanne's shoes?**

❺ **List some positive and negative outcomes in this situation.**

Aber Education

39

Activity 20

Discussion Cards (c)

☞ Scenario 5

Michelle has been learning the piano since she was six years old. When Michelle's family moved into another suburb, Michelle had to attend a different school and also had to get a new piano teacher. The piano teacher lived about five minutes drive from Michelle's house and picked Michelle up from school before her lesson. Michelle's mother or father would then come and pick Michelle up from the teacher's house when the lesson was over. Michelle really likes learning the piano but her teacher has started to become very strange. He is asking Michelle weird questions about whether she is interested in boys and asks if boys make certain comments. He has even asked if they touch her and wanted Michelle to show him. The questions make Michelle very embarrassed and they seem to have nothing to do with the piano. The piano teacher always tells Michelle that their conversations are secret to be kept between them only.

Michelle really wants to keep learning the piano and it was so hard for her mother to find her a good piano teacher after the move. She doesn't want her mum to have to worry about all of that again. She never knows what her piano teacher is going to come out with, or worse, what he may do!

☞ FOCUS QUESTIONS:

❶   **How did you feel about this story?**

❷   **What would you do if you were Michelle?**

❸   **Have you ever been in a situation like this?**

❹   **How did you handle it?**

❺   **Who might you talk to about this issue?**
(E.g. your friends, your parents, your school teacher, your piano teacher?)

❻   **What could be a positive outcome in this situation?**

☞ Scenario 6

When Stephanie was seven her mother married for the second time. Steph's step-father John, was younger than her mother and was quite a lot of fun to have around. In the last few years, John has become angry and violent towards Steph's mother. Most of the time, Steph tries to ignore their shouting and arguments with each other, however, it is getting to the point where Steph cannot stand it any longer. When Steph woke up one morning, she noticed her mother had a big red mark on her cheek which later turned into a bruise. Steph's mum said she had banged into a door when she got up in the middle of the night. Her step-father had gone to work early.

☞ FOCUS QUESTIONS:

❶ **What do you think Steph should do?**

❷ **Who might Steph be able to talk to about what is going on?**

❸ **Who would you talk to about a problem like this?**

❹ **If you were one of Stephanie's friends, how might you be able to help this situation?**

Activity 21 | # Discussion Cards (d)

☞ Scenario 7

Christy is in Year 6 and has started mixing with some of the kids at the high school on weekends. She thinks that this will make finding friends at high school a bit easier as most of her close friends in Year 7 are going off to different schools.

At first it was kind of cool to be hanging out with the older kids but they have started getting involved in things that Christy isn't so keen on. Last week three of the guys in the gang vandalised her primary school. Although Christy wasn't involved in any way, she has heard the boys bragging about it and has seen the damage that they caused. Some of the students in Christy's school have had their work destroyed as the boys have sprayed graffiti all over a mural.

One of the older kids has warned Christy that if she dobs on them she will regret it big time! They have told her they will make high school a nightmare for her.

☞ FOCUS QUESTIONS:

❶ What would you do if you were Christy?

❷ Who would you talk to about this?

❸ What would you say to the older kids?

❹ How could this problem be resolved?

☞ Scenario 8

Macy is thirteen and comes from a large family. Her older brother has just been sent to gaol for stealing cars. Her parents never seem to notice her and her other brothers and sisters are always fighting. Macy is not getting a lot of sleep at home and her school work is really suffering. Some of the kids in Macy's class tease her because she always turns up for school looking very scruffy. The kids also tease her about her family. Macy has told you that she is sick and tired of everything and that there is nothing good in her life. She also said that she can't take much more of things and that she thinks everything is just going to get worse.

☞ FOCUS QUESTIONS:

❶ What might Macy be thinking about doing?

❷ What would you say to Macy?

❸ What are Macy's options?

❹ What are your options?

❺ What could be a positive outcome in this situation?

Activity 22 | Discussion Cards (e)

☞ Scenario 9

Marcus is twelve years old. His mother and father got divorced when he was seven and he sees his dad every second weekend. Marcus is very angry about the divorce and doesn't get on very well with his mother who he blames for the break up. Marcus does well at school but has trouble when it comes to sport or anything where he has to work in a group. He has a very short temper and gets extremely angry over small things. No one has seen Marcus smile for a long time. He never seems to find anything funny and always seem impatient with everyone. While Marcus has always been fairly popular with the other boys in his class, he is slowly driving his friends away as they can't be bothered putting up with his mood swings and rages.

☞ FOCUS QUESTIONS:

❶ What can you say to Marcus?

❷ If you were Marcus, where could you get help?

❸ What could be a positive outcome in this situation?

☞ Scenario 10

Louise lives on the same street as Angie and also sits next to her in class. Angie is very good at her schoolwork and is also an excellent basketballer. Louise is annoyed that Angie is popular at school, good at her work AND good at sport. Louise has told you that she doesn't think it is fair that Angie should be really good at everything when she herself isn't really good at anything. Louise has started leaving anonymous notes around for Angie to find. She writes the notes with her left hand so that Angie can't recognise the handwriting. The notes are really mean, saying horrible things about Angie's appearance and that the other kids don't really like her. Although you have no proof, you suspect Louise is sending the notes as she has made it clear to you that she is jealous of Angie's achievements.

☞ FOCUS QUESTIONS:

❶ What would you do in this situation?

❷ What would you say to Angie?

❸ Who would you talk to?

❹ What could be a positive outcome in this situation?

Activity 23 | # Discussion Cards (f)

☞ Your Scenario

In your group, talk about some problems that individual group members may be facing either at school or at home. You will each get a chance to talk about your problem.

NOTE: You DO NOT have to talk about a problem if you do not want to.

You may want to talk about:

- ❑ Bullying in the playground or on the bus
- ❑ Problems at home with family members
- ❑ Problems out of school with other kids
- ❑ Feeling sad or angry about something
- ❑ Worrying about changes that you have no control over,
  e.g. parents getting divorced, moving to a new school, someone dying.

☞ FOCUS QUESTIONS:

Answer the questions using the space below to clarify thoughts and group ideas. Work through a problem solving process as a group. Use the back of this page if you need more room to write your notes.

❶ **What is the issue?**

❷ **What are the options available?**

❸ **What are the positive consequences for each option?**

❹ **What are the negative consequences for each option?**

❺ **What is the best option?**

❻ **What conclusions did your group come to about this problem?**

❼ **What conclusions did YOU come to about this problem?**

Write your notes here: _____

_____

_____

_____

_____

_____

Activity 24 | # Discussion Cards: Reflection

❶ What number scenario was your group discussing?

_____

❷ What were the issues involved in this scenario?

_____

_____

❸ What is your experience with such a story like this? Discuss.

(e.g. Have you, or someone you know, been involved in a similar situation?)

_____

_____

_____

❹ How was this situation resolved?

_____

_____

Working in a group

❺ How did you feel about how your group dealt with this problem?

_____

_____

❻ Did you mainly agree / disagree with other group members? Discuss.

_____

_____

❼ How much do you think you contributed in your group?

_____

_____

Self-Assessment: Rubric

☞ Complete the rubric below:

	YES	NO
Our group stayed on the topic.	❑	❑
Everyone had a chance to say what he/she thought.	❑	❑
I was happy with my input into the group	❑	❑
We listened to each person's opinion.	❑	❑
Our group came to an agreement.	❑	❑
Each member of our group had a special role.	❑	❑
I felt uncomfortable in this group.	❑	❑